Midwest
PIE

Recipes that shaped a region

T0267818

More Cookbooks from
Belt Publishing

The Belt Cookie Table Cookbook

The Pocket Pawpaw Cookbook

Rust Belt Vegan Kitchen

Midwest
PIE

Recipes that shaped a region

Edited by Meredith Pangrace
Introduction by Phoebe Mogharei

Belt Publishing

Printed in the United States of America
First edition 2023
1 2 3 4 5 6 7 8 9

ISBN: 9781953368522

Belt Publishing
13443 Detroit Ave., Ste. 2
Lakewood, OH 44107
www.beltpublishing.com

Cover and book design by Meredith Pangrace

Amish Shoo Fly Pies displayed in Lancaster, Pennsylvania, 1980.

Table of Contents

Regional Favorites

"Desperation" Pies

Midwestern Ingredients

Retro Favorites

Handheld Pies

INTRODUCTION

Phoebe Mogharei

"I ate apple pie and ice cream—it was getting better as I got
deeper into Iowa, the pie bigger, the ice cream richer."
—Jack Kerouac, *On the Road*

In the small Iowa town where I attended college, there was,
naturally, a local diner. It was much like the diners you'd find
in many small midwestern towns, though it was set apart by its
hodgepodge of inexplicable décor. Manhattan skylines were etched
into the glass separating the booths. There were faux Italian frescoes
with background colors that didn't match the restaurant's gray walls.
And a Turkish tourism poster sat next to other saturated landscapes
of agricultural scenes. The place certainly wasn't fancy—a dinner
with soup, side, and a dessert cost around $8—but it had character.
And if anything, the lack of a cohesive interior sensibility made me
trust the people who ran it, as if it was a sure sign their priority was
cooking, not interior design.

But in the corner, between the kitchen and the hallway that
led back to the bathroom, was something that looked expensive,
almost futuristic: the pie case. Tier after tier of shelves lit up like a
marquee, the glass case showcased slices of pie—lemon meringue,
apple, chocolate cream—as if they were precious crown jewels.
The pie wasn't expensive or pretentious, but it was always there,
always on display, and always plentiful. There was never any doubt
as to what you would choose when it came time to order dessert.

Throughout the American Midwest, pie is so omnipresent
it often goes unnoticed, or at least unremarked upon. The fact
that you can get it at almost any small-town diner around the

region, with or without the pomp of a rotating pie case, makes it different from many other desserts. And while New Englanders have historically claimed the food as their own, the Midwest has its own special and enduring relationship with the homey dessert. It's been there since the covered-wagon days, taking cues from traditions that originated in immigrants' motherlands and creating a unique regional legacy of its own. *Midwest Pie: Recipes that Shaped a Region* is a way to honor those legacies and help bring them to life in your own kitchen, midwestern or otherwise.

To better understand how pie found its place in the Midwest, it's helpful to first understand how it found its way to the New World. Pie originally came to the United States from England with the first colonists, though we know now that pumpkin pie probably wasn't on offer at the first Thanksgiving in Plymouth. Most of these prerevolutionary British pies were savory—often filled with ox tongue, mutton, or the meat of small fowl—and the crusts were called, appetizingly, "coffins." Usually a simple mixture of water and flour or some other grain—no fat—coffins were cut in thick slabs that became rock hard during the cooking process. They worked as resealable airtight storage containers that preserved the filling, though they were not meant to be eaten. According to pie historian Janet Clarkson, despite their toughness, it's unlikely these coffins were totally discarded, however; more likely, they were reused or soaked in sauce until they were finally soft enough to chew without cracking a tooth.[1]

Amelia Simmons's *American Cookery*, the first cookbook published stateside, appeared in 1796, and it included several pie recipes. Lots of these were savory as well, though Simmons also wrote instructions for an apple pie and a pumpkin pudding that could be set in a crust. The crust recipes contained a good amount of butter, making them more like the pies we know today.[2] In these early colonial days, pies were practical foods: they created their own gravy and could be a complete meal on their own. They also gave bakers an easy way to use odds and ends, leftovers, and dried produce. It was the perfect culinary standby for Yankees who liked to think of themselves as thrifty, pragmatic, and full of common sense.

But by the mid-nineteenth century, pie had become much more than a practicality. It was a favorite breakfast of Ralph Waldo Emerson, and some people ate it three times a day.[3] One British journalist visiting the East Coast wrote that "an unholy appetite for Pie works untold woes" in the American people, thereby cementing the new country's love for pie as a nationalist snub of the stuffy Brits.[4] Mark Twain was known to deal with depressive episodes by eating half a huckleberry pie and drinking a quart of milk.[5] Rudyard Kipling, who lived outside Brattleboro, Vermont, between 1892 and 1896, somewhat derisively called New England "the Great Pie Belt" due to the dish's prominent position in the region.[6] Locals (forgive the pun) ate the moniker up.

As America expanded, and as new states took shape west of the Appalachians, pie moved west as well. The dish was portable and versatile, which gave it lasting appeal. When Civil War mess cooks couldn't get apples, they'd just substitute hardtack and sugar to make a mock version. (Up until the 1990s, Ritz also included a recipe on the side of their boxes for mock apple pie using their crackers.[7]) For pioneers on the trail, pies were handy for the same reason they had been in the colonies: they could be made with dried ingredients, and unlike bread, they could bake in a Dutch oven over a simple fire. As more Europeans settled in the Midwest, they found that local ingredients like chokecherries (page 88), persimmons (page 102), and black walnuts (page 83) could all be incorporated into a pie at will to make something delicious. In 1851, a Norwegian immigrant living in Beloit, Wisconsin, penned a letter home that read, "Strawberries, raspberries, and blackberries thrive here. From these they make a wonderful dish combined with syrup and sugar, which is called 'pai.' I can tell you that is something that glides easily down your throat; they also make the same sort of pai out of apples or finely ground meat, with syrup added, and that is really the most superb."[8]

By the early twentieth century, the dessert suffered some from the emergence of the nutritional science field; it turns out that eating pie three times a day might not be the surest path toward long-term health. But Americans weren't able to kick their addiction so easily. One apocryphal *New York Times* editorial waxed delirious, declaring, "Pie is the food of the heroic. No pie-eating people can be permanently vanquished."[9] According to food writer Matt Siegel, a writer for the *Milwaukee Journal Sentinel* weighed in on the debate over the national flower by arguing that Americans shouldn't be wasting time discussing plants when pie could easily serve as the national emblem.[10] Even American English reflected the culture's love for the pastry, and this era birthed some of our more common pie-related idioms, including "easy as pie," which refers to how easy it was to eat the dessert (as opposed to making it), and "pie in the sky," a phrase coined by IWW labor activist Joe Hill to mock the idea of toiling on earth for the promise of later sweet rewards in heaven.

Midwesterners had their own important role to play in this history of pie in America. As more women entered the workforce after World War I, baking, especially for multistep desserts like pies, decreased significantly because there simply wasn't someone at home who could dedicate the time to it. Farm wives throughout the Midwest, though, continued baking pies as always, creating an unbroken family tradition of pie making that was becoming less common in cities and more industrial towns.[11]

Many of those pies were cream- and dairy-based, the types of pies the Midwest is now known for in particular. Hoosier cream pie (page 71), an example of a "desperation pie" that involves a simple recipe of pantry staples and a healthy dose of cream, is an Indiana icon. Similarly, Shoofly pie (page 75) is associated with the Pennsylvania Dutch and made with molasses, giving it its signature deep treacly brown color.

But the region has other beloved pies as well. Rhubarb pie (page 104) isn't strictly midwestern, but it's become a regional staple. The tart stalks, which were also called "pie plants," thrive in the Midwest's cold winters and milder summers, and bakers used them to make what was winkingly called a "dear pie" because of the amount of pricey sugar that was needed to counteract the stalks' tartness. In her Little House novel *The First Four Years*, Laura Ingalls Wilder writes about the early days of her marriage when she accidentally forgets to add sugar to a rhubarb pie. A quick-witted and tactful dinner guest kindly announces that he prefers it when hosts let the guests add sugar to their own slices.[12] Though pumpkin pie (page 53) certainly isn't unique to the Midwest either, it is nevertheless championed by it. It's the state pie of Illinois, which produces the most pumpkins in the country and is the home of Libby's, the classic brand of canned pumpkin.[13]

After World War II, many women returned to homemaking in large numbers, and advancing industrialization and kitchen hacks that were meant to make cooking and housekeeping easier abounded. Several such innovations—pudding mixes, canned fruit, and frozen crusts—directly affected the pie-making process, and the Midwest once again found itself at the forefront of innovation. At the vanguard of the frozen pie market was Pet-Ritz, a company that grew out of a roadside cherry pie stand in Michigan. They first started freezing pies individually so tourists could take them back home, but they soon graduated to a commercial scale and then branched out to selling premade frozen pie crusts. They eventually came under the umbrella of the Pillsbury Company.[14]

But even as shortcut ingredients like these became readily available to home bakers, pies made completely from scratch were still seen as something special. In *American Cuisine*, Paul Freeman notes that in twentieth-century community cookbooks, desserts were the one category that did not fall victim to "the relentless twentieth-century drive for convenience." As he writes, "It was fine to use canned string beans for a vegetable course and employ canned cream soup as a sauce base, but until the late 1950s, baking from scratch was expected from contributors to local compendia. In a sample of thirty-three community cookbooks from the Great Plains, all dating from the 1970s, half the space is taken up by desserts."[15]

Making a lovingly baked dessert from scratch was a way for women to both show off their creativity and skill and a way to connect with their neighbors. Community cookbooks, for example, can be sourced to the Civil War, when they were sold to financially support dependents of deceased Union soldiers.[16] Protestant church groups regularly put out regional anthologies to raise money for church repairs, improvements, or other ventures. *Buckeye Cookery and Practical Housekeeping*, first published in 1877, was assembled by the women of the First Congregational Church in Marysville, Ohio, and eventually sold more than eighty thousand copies. Better known as the *Buckeye Cookbook*, the collection is dedicated to "the Plucky Housewives of 1876, who master their work instead of allowing it to master them" and contains tips on everything from drinks to floral arrangements. It also includes recipes for both baked and stewed "pie plant."[17]

Junior leagues, women's social organizations that were "committed to promoting voluntarism, developing the potential of women, and improving communities," were also no strangers to pie making.[18] First started by Mary Harriman Rumsey, a Barnard graduate who had been inspired by the settlement movement, the regional chapters became well-known for their annual fundraising cookbooks. Pies were similarly a big part of local, county, and state fairs. While competitive portions of summer fairs traditionally centered around agriculture, state fairs soon began to have "women's work" shows; the Wisconsin State Fair held its first in 1889.[19] Since then, baked goods and other activities that would conventionally fall under the banner of "homemaking" have become staples at these events.

In this way, we can see how pie making, cookbooks, and baking competitions played a significant social role, particularly for women in the Midwest. Junior league cookbooks became one way, albeit limited, to monetize, record, and distribute women's creative endeavors. Fair competitions offered a rare opportunity for women to publicly showcase their skills as well.

Fair competitions and junior leagues would have been largely white affairs throughout most of the twentieth century, but pie has also played an important role for communities of color in the region. Bean pie, for example, came to prominence through the Nation of Islam, the Black nationalist organization founded in Detroit and associated with figures like Malcolm X and Muhammad Ali. Followers prioritized a rejection of slavery's legacy, and soul food, which had its roots in communities of enslaved people in the South, was disparaged. Elijah Muhammad, the Nation of Islam's leader between 1934 and 1975, set out dietary rules that were centered on both Islam and nutrition: no pork or alcohol, and, interestingly, no beans besides navy beans. Navy bean pie (page 57), often seen as an alternative to the creamy sweet potato pie in the South, became a staple in and beyond Detroit. And according to Rossi Anastopoulo in *Taste*, just like junior leagues and church groups, members of the Nation of Islam used it as a fundraising tool.[20]

Manoomin pie (page 94) is another sweet pie made with a typically savory ingredient. "Manoomin," which refers to the wild rice (actually a cereal grain) native to the Great Lakes region, was harvested and tended by the Ojibwe people. Ojibwe lore describes how their ancestors were told to travel to where food grows on water—a place they found in the cold northern lakes of the region. You may recognize manoomin as the plaintiff in a 2021 case brought against the Minnesota Department of National Resources to fight against Enbridge Line 3, one of the largest crude oil pipelines in the world.[21] Manoomin was given legally enforceable rights by tribal authority, allowing the grain itself (through the intermediary of the White Earth Band) to sue the state.[22] That the manoomin itself is seen as a vital member of the community, with its own rights, is another particularly profound example of the ways food sources and local crops have crucially come to define midwestern cuisines and cultural identities.

While pie may not be as predominant as it once was, its history and role in the Midwest is still evolving. Roadside stands and family-run companies continue to use their time-tested recipes. Wick's Pies, in the small town of Winchester, Indiana, is a not-so-small operation that churns out around 10,000 pies (many of them their famous Hoosier pies) every eight hours.[23] New shops, with new missions and flavors—like Justice of the Pies, whose mission includes a fight against food apartheid and food insecurity on Chicago's West Side—are also opening and thriving.

The pies in this collection, minimally updated from their original historical sources, are as varied as the history of pie in the region itself: made from local fruits, meat, dairy, nuts, and pantry staples. The bulk of the recipes are for beloved sweet pies, with some more savory fare sprinkled in as well, such as the pasties taken to work by ore miners in Michigan's Upper Peninsula. Along with the recipes, you'll find helpful tips and historical snippets to help give a little background on each individual pie. Don't be afraid to play around—there was a time when there were as many types of pies at a midwestern gathering as there were women, each with a signature treat. Whether these recipes bring back long-lost memories of your grandmother's kitchen or whether they're completely brand-new to you, there's a little something here for everyone. And hopefully, as you work your way through the following pages, you'll find something that reminds you and your loved ones of home and family, and maybe something that even feels worthy of a coveted spot in that small-town diner pie case.

NOTES

[1] Janet Clarkson, *Pie: A Global History* (Reaktion Books, 2009).

[2] Amelia Simmons, *American Cookery* (Hudson & Goodwin, 1796).

[3] "The Pie Microbe," *New York Times*, July 23, 1884.

[4] Matt Siegel, *The Secret History of Food: Strange but True Stories about the Origins of Everything We Eat* (Ecco Press, 2021).

[5] Helen McCully and Eleanor Noderer, eds., *The American Heritage Cookbook* (American Heritage Press, 1969).

[6] "The Great Pie Belt," *The Cambridge Tribune*, November 23, 1895.

[7] Margie Williamson, "Dishing Up Memories: Ritz Cracker Pie or Mock Apple Pie?" *Now Habersham*, November 18, 2020.

[8] McCully and Noderer, *The American Heritage Cookbook*.

[9] "Pie," *New York Times*, May 3, 1902.

[10] Siegel, *The Secret History of Food*.

[11] Andrew F. Smith, ed., *Oxford Encyclopedia of Food and Drink in America* (Oxford University Press, second edition, 2012).

[12] Laura Ingalls Wilder, *The First Four Years* (HarperCollins, 2008).

[13] "Pumpkins: Background & Statistics," USDA, Economic Research Service, last updated November 17, 2022, https://www.ers.usda.gov/newsroom/trending-topics/pumpkins-background-statistics/.

[14] Lynne Olver, "FAQs: Pie & Pastry," The Food Timeline, https://www.foodtimeline.org/foodpies.html.

[15] Paul Freedman, *American Cuisine: And How It Got This Way* (Liveright Publishing Corporation, 2019).

[16] Lynne Ireland, "The Compiled Cookbook as Foodways Autobiography," *Western Folklore* 40, no. 1, January 1981.

[17] *Buckeye Cookery and Practical Housekeeping* (Buckeye Publishing Company, 1877).

[18] "Mission, Visions & Values," Junior League of Ann Arbor, accessed October 2022, https://www.jlaa.org/about/mission-vision-values/.

[19] "History of Wisconsin State Fair," accessed October 2022, https://wistatefair.com/fair/history/.

[20] Rossi Anastopoulo, "The Radical Pie That Fueled a Nation," *Taste*, November 13, 2018.

[21] *Manoomin v. Minnesota Department of Natural Resources* (2021).

[22] Eamon Whalen, "The Latest Attempt to Stop Line 3 Hits a Snag in Tribal Court," *Mother Jones*, April 6, 2022.

[23] "About," Wick's Pies, accessed December 2022, https://www.wickspies.com/about/.

An Amish crafts store on Lincoln Highway in Lancaster County, Pennsylvania. Built in 1946, it is famous for Shoo Fly Pie.

Photo courtesy Mike Druckenbrod, 2013

EDITOR'S NOTE
Meredith Pangrace

This recipe collection aims to introduce you to several pies unique to the Midwest region and to reintroduce you to classic favorites with a unique twist or shortcut. I selected most of the recipes by scouring thrift stores for old community cookbooks to see which ones repeatedly appeared as favorites. I found others in old family notebooks and recipe-card boxes.

If you enjoy any kind of cooking or baking, I highly recommend searching for recipes this way. Yes, nowadays you can find recipes for almost anything online, but the spiral-bound gems you stumble across in used bookshops and thrift stores give you a fascinating window into the time and culture of their origin. For example, when I came across a recipe for Star-Spangled Cherry Pie, I could picture the cook, the kitchen, and even the music playing in the background as the pie chilled in the Frigidaire. My mind conjured up a completely different scenario when I came across the directions for Sawdust Pie. These recipes didn't ask me to read a ten-paragraph blog introduction about them; in fact, both of them were no more than fifty words long. But I was able to use my imagination to fill in the story behind them. (And neither of them came up in a Google search, so don't bother looking!)

Many of the recipes for these types of pies emerged out of hard times—the hardscrabble experiences of immigrants dealing with harsh Midwest winters, or families looking for ways to save resources during the Great Depression or World War II. While some recipes tried to disguise their humble aspirations with names like Millionaire Pie, others, such as Vinegar Pie, kept it honest. This quality is actually an asset to you as you try the recipes. If they fail, it won't be a huge financial loss, and it's easy to just try again. The most expensive ingredient you'll need will most likely be the half gallon of vanilla ice cream you buy to serve on the side. (While not specifically noted on all the recipes, the majority of these pies are enhanced by a side of ice cream.)

These recipes and accompanying instructions aren't designed to turn you into a master pie baker by any means. Most of them consist of humble pantry ingredients and simple techniques. With much respect to the master pie bakers, the beautiful glossy cookbook writers, and those who run stunning social media accounts, a pie does not have to be worthy of a magazine cover in order for it be enjoyed while it's being assembled or consumed. An ugly pie—and yes, there are definitely a few ugly ones in this collection—is perhaps the most endearing pie of all. And unless it's burned to a crisp (try at least not to do that, please), the amount of butter and sugar in them will usually save the taste, if not the form.

Finally, do not be afraid to make a pie. The generations before us made them without fancy tools, ice cold kitchens, or pages of detailed instructions. Most importantly, they made pies without fear. And you can too (well, at least *these* particular ones . . .).

Good luck, and happy baking!

A Brief Introduction on Pie Crusts . . .

If you're new to making pie dough, don't expect a perfect crust on your first try. The dough can be finnicky, oven temperature controls vary, and so-called "no-fail" techniques are highly debated. You'll most likely need to practice a bit first before you find exactly what works for you.

Most vintage cookbooks assume the reader has an existing knowledge of pie crust that's been passed down by generations, so they often include simple three-sentence instructions for making dough such as:

Mix flour and salt.

Cut in lard.

Add water one spoon at a time.

In contrast, modern pie cookbooks tend to contain pages and pages of detailed rules and instructions. The former is cryptic, the latter can be completely overwhelming.

So if you're intimidated by the entire process, there is no shame in using a premade crust. And there are plenty of recipes in this collection that use alternatives like cookie crusts and "mix-in-the-pan" crusts. But here are a few simple tips to keep in mind if this is your first foray into the world of pie making.

Tips for Mixing Traditional Pie Dough

The ingredients for a pie crust like a cold environment. If your kitchen is warm, chill your flour as well as your fat, and keep your water ice-cold. Try to work quickly so everything stays cool.

Don't worry if you don't have a pastry blender. Most bakers prefer working with their hands when mixing dough, finding it easier to get the desired pea-sized crumbs. Just remember to run your hands under cold water for a bit first to make sure they are not too warm.

Roll out your dough on a pastry cloth if you have trouble transferring it from the work surface to the pie pan.

To help achieve an even thickness, first form your dough into a thick disc shape, then roll from the center out, not quite to the edge.

Make sure your crust is rolled out evenly, about 1/8- to 1/4-inch thick, and large enough to cover the entire bottom of your pan and drape over the sides and trim.

If you're "blind baking" (baking the crust first before filling it), cover the dough with foil once it's in the pie pan and pour in dried beans to weigh it down so that the crust maintains its shape. Be sure to wait until the crust is cooled before filling.

Tips for Baking the Crust

Beginners may like to start by baking their pie crusts in Pyrex pie pans because they allow you to see the browning through the glass, but the best pie pans are dark metal, which allow for even baking.

When baking fruit pies, put a cookie sheet on the lower rack to catch any overflow.

If a crust is getting too brown and the filling is not cooked, cover the exposed crust with foil.

Brushing the top or bottom crust with egg white will give it a nice, brown sheen.

Troubleshooting

If your pastry crust is too crumbly, the flour and fat might have been overmixed.

If your pastry crust is tough, the dough might have been too wet (you used too much water) or overmixed.

If your crust is soggy, the oven temperature could have been too low or the pie was cooled too quickly.

If your crust is baked unevenly, it could be because your dough was not rolled to a uniform thickness.

When working with your pie dough, if it is too soft or crumbly, the fat may not be chilled enough.

A Few Simple Crust Recipes

"Never-Fail" Pie Crust

Makes 2 large crusts

Ingredients
- 3 cups flour (sifted)
- 1 teaspoon salt
- 1 cup lard
- 1 egg
- 5 tablespoons water
- 1 tablespoon vinegar

Instructions
1. In a large bowl, mix the flour, salt, and lard with your hands until crumbly.

2. In a separate bowl, beat the egg with the vinegar and water.

3. Mix into the flour mixture.

4. Divide into two parts and let rest 30 minutes to 1 hour before rolling out.

Baked Single (One-Crust) Pie Shell

Makes 1 crust, when recipe calls for a single baked shell

Ingredients
1 1/3 cups flour
1/2 teaspoon salt
1/2 cup shortening
3 tablespoons water

Instructions
1. Preheat oven to 475°F.

2. In a large bowl, mix the flour, salt, and shortening with your hands until crumbly.

3. Sprinkle with water and mix with fork.

4. Form into a ball, then roll out to be 1 inch larger than your inverted pie pan.

5. Gently ease crust into the pan. Scallop the edges, using your fingers to create a continuous wave.

6. Prick the bottom of the crust with a fork. Bake for 8 minutes.

Standard Pastry for a Two-Crust Pie

Makes 2 crusts, when recipe calls for a bottom shell and top crust

Ingredients
2 cups flour
1 teaspoon salt
2/3 cup shortening
4 tablespoons water

Instructions
1. Preheat oven to 475°F.

2. In a large bowl, mix the flour, salt, and shortening with your hands until crumbly.

3. Sprinkle with water and mix with fork.

4. Divide the dough in half. Form one half into a ball, then roll out to be 1 inch larger than your inverted pie pan.

5. Gently ease crust into the pan.

6. Roll out the second dough, which will be ready to be placed on top of the pie after filling.

7. Bake according to pie recipe's instructions.

No-Roll "Instant" Pie Crust

Makes one 9-inch crust

Ingredients
   1 1/2 cups flour
   1 tablespoon sugar
   1/2 teaspoon salt
   1/2 cup oil
   1 tablespoon milk

Instructions
1.   Preheat oven to 425°F.

2.   In a large bowl, mix all the ingredients together with a fork.

3.   Press the dough into a microwave-safe pie pan.

4.   Bake for 12–15 minutes.

5.   Microwave for 4 minutes. Let cool before filling.

Cookie Crust

Makes one 9-inch crust

A few recipes in this collection call for a graham cracker crust, but crushed chocolate sandwich cookies, gingersnaps, or even pecan sandies will work. Chill the crust to set it, or if you prefer a bit of a toasted flavor, bake the crust for no more than 10 minutes at 350°F.

Makes 1 crust

Ingredients
- 1 3/4 cups cookie crumbs
- 5 tablespoons butter (melted)

Instructions
1. Combine the ingredients and press into a 9-inch pie pan.

Pies

Old
Classics

Angel Pie

Originating around the 1930s, angel pies are unique in the fact that the filling is poured into a meringue crust rather than having a meringue top. The name of the pie is appropriate, as the lovely filling appears to be floating high above the clouds. Many classic angel pie recipes do not include nuts and cracker crumbs, yet their addition here adds a welcome flavor and texture.

This pie needs to firm up in the refrigerator overnight, so plan ahead when making it.

Makes 1 pie

Ingredients

For the meringue crust:

3 egg whites
1 teaspoon baking powder
1 cup sugar
1 cup chopped walnuts
1/2 cup cracker crumbs
Pinch of salt

For the filling:

4 egg yolks
1/2 cup sugar
3 tablespoons lemon juice
2 tablespoons lemon rind
1 cup whipping cream

Instructions

1. Preheat the oven to 300°F and grease a pie pan.

2. Make the meringue crust: beat egg whites until stiff.

3. Add baking powder, salt, and sugar and beat again.

4. Gently fold in the nuts and cracker crumbs.

5. Spread the meringue into the pie pan.

6. Bake for 40 minutes.

7. Make the filling: beat the egg yolks.

8. Add the sugar, lemon juice, and lemon rind.

9. Cook the mixture in a double boiler until thickened. Then set aside to cool.

10. Whip the cream until stiff.

11. When meringue crust is finished baking and cooling, spread one half of the whipped cream onto the crust.

12. Spread the cooled filling onto the crust, followed by the remaining whipped cream.

13. Chill for 24 hours.

Bob Andy Pie

The warm spices of this Amish custard pie make it unique. While one might assume it is named after a well-respected pie-loving Bob in the community, it's actually said to be named after two favored castrated workhorses.

Makes 2 pies

Ingredients
2 unbaked pie shells

For the filling:
1 cup granulated sugar
1 cup brown sugar
3 eggs, separated
1 1/2 tablespoons butter (melted)
1/2 teaspoon ground cloves
3 heaping tablespoons flour
1 1/4 cups whole milk
1 14-ounce can sweetened condensed milk
1 teaspoon ground cinnamon

Instructions
1. Preheat oven to 440°F.

2. In a large bowl, mix the sugar, flour, cinnamon, and cloves.

3. In a separate bowl, beat the egg yolks. Add the butter and the two types of milk.

4. Stir the wet mixture into the dry mixture.

5. Beat egg whites until stiff peaks form. Fold the egg whites into the filling.

6. Quickly pour the mixture into the two unbaked pie shells evenly so the spices do not settle.

7. Bake for 10–15 minutes.

8. Lower the oven temperature to 325°F and bake an additional 30–45 minutes or until the centers are set.

Kitchen inside the farmhouse at Yoder's Amish Home, an authentic Amish farm that began accepting visitors in 1983 near Walnut Creek in central Ohio, along the "Amish Country Byway."

Photograph in the Carol M. Highsmith Archive, Library of Congress, Prints and Photographs Division.

Butterscotch Pie

Butterscotch usually reminds us of instant pudding in the school cafeteria or the candy Grandpa kept in his glove compartment, but the real flavor of an old-fashioned butterscotch pie is a whole new experience.

Makes 1 pie

Ingredients
   1 baked pie shell

   For the filling:
   2 tablespoons butter (melted)
   1 cup brown sugar
   4 tablespoons milk + 1 cup milk
   1 egg yolk
   1 tablespoon cornstarch

   1 cup whipped cream

Instructions
1. In a large bowl, mix the butter, brown sugar, and 4 tablespoons of milk.

2. In a saucepan, beat the egg yolk. Stir in the cornstarch and remaining milk. Bring to a boil over medium heat. Remove from heat and let cool.

3. Once cooled, pour the mixture from the saucepan into the butter and brown sugar mixture. Whisk together until smooth.

4. Pour the mixture into the baked pie shell.

5. Chill in the refrigerator for 2–4 hours.

6. Serve chilled with whipped cream.

Farmer with his wife and child eating pie at pie supper, 1940.
Pie suppers were fundraisers that auctioned off pies to raise money,
most often for schools or churches.

Photograph by Russell Lee, Library of Congress, Prints and Photographs Division.

Funeral Pie

From the Pennsylvania Dutch comes this *rosine* (the German word for "raisin") pie, traditionally brought to wakes. Raisins were always kept on hand, so this pie could be made at short notice.

Makes 1 pie

Ingredients
1 unbaked pie shell

For the filling:
2 cups raisins
1 cup water
1 cup orange juice
1 cup sugar
3 tablespoons cornstarch
1 1/2 teaspoons ground cinnamon
1 cup coarsely chopped walnuts
1 tablespoon apple cider vinegar
3 tablespoons unsalted butter
Pinch of salt

Instructions
1. Preheat oven to 400°F.

2. In a medium saucepan, cook the raisins with the water and orange juice over medium heat until raisins are plump and soft.

3. Reduce heat to low and stir in the sugar, cornstarch, and spices. Continue stirring, and cook until the mixture gets thick and starts to bubble a bit.

4. Remove pan from heat. Stir in the nuts, salt, vinegar, and butter.

5. Bake 25–30 minutes until golden brown.

6. Cool to set.

Mennonite and Pennsylvania Dutch children purchase candy and baked goods at a farm auction, Lancaster County, Pennsylvania, 1942.

Impossible Pie

For bakers in a hurry or who find themselves without a premade crust in sight, this creamy pie with a crunchy coconut topping "impossibly" creates its own crust. While this recipe is based on old Amish recipes, versions with the same moniker appeared much later. They were a very different style of pie, using cornmeal or Bisquick for the crust, and they included savory versions (such as cheeseburger and taco.)

Makes 1 pie

Ingredients
2 eggs
1 cup milk
3 1/2 ounces of sweetened shredded coconut
1/4 cup flour
1 teaspoon vanilla
1/2 teaspoon baking powder
2 teaspoons melted butter, plus butter to grease a 9-inch pie pan
5/8 cup sugar
Pinch of salt

Instructions
1. Preheat oven to 350°F.

2. Butter a 9-inch pie pan.

3. In a large bowl, beat the eggs.

4. Add all the remaining ingredients and mix well. Pour into the pie pan.

5. Bake for 40–50 minutes until set.

6. Cool and refrigerate for a few hours to fully set.

Millionaire Pie

Ironically named, this pie is made of very middle-class ingredients and can be made in minutes if using a prepared crust.

Makes 1 pie

Ingredients
1 graham cracker crust

For the filling:
1 8-ounce package of cream cheese (softened)
2 cups powdered sugar
1 cup crushed pineapple (drained and chilled)
1 1/2 cups prepared whipped topping (such as Cool Whip)

Chopped walnuts and maraschino cherries (with stems) for decoration

Instructions
1. Beat the cream cheese with the powdered sugar.

2. Blend in the chilled pineapple and mix to combine.

3. Fold in the whipped topping.

4. Spread into the graham cracker crust.

5. Sprinkle with nuts and chill.

6. Add cherries before serving.

Sawdust Pie

The Amish truly had a very direct way of naming their pies. You'd expect a very dry pie with this recipe, but it's actually the shredded coconut that's the source of the name.

Makes 1 pie

Ingredients
    1 unbaked pie shell

For the filling:
    1 1/2 cups shredded coconut
    1 1/2 cups graham cracker crumbs
    1 1/2 cups chopped pecans
    1 1/2 cups sugar
    1 cup egg whites (from about 4 to 5 eggs)

Instructions
1. Preheat oven to 350°F.

2. In a large bowl, mix the coconut, graham cracker crumbs, pecans, and sugar.

3. Beat the egg whites, just until foamy.

4. Add the eggs to the rest of the filling.

5. Pour the mixture into the unbaked pie shell.

6. Bake for 35–40 minutes. If the top starts to look too brown, cover with foil.

7. Cool to set the filling.

Schnitz Pie

This pie gets its name from the German word for "sliced." It's a traditional Amish pie made of sliced and dried fruit, mainly apples.

Makes 1 pie

Ingredients
2 unbaked pie shells

For the filling:
3 cups dried apples
2 cups warm water
2/3 cup sugar
1/4 teaspoon cloves
1/2 teaspoon cinnamon

Cream and coarse sugar to brush on the top crust

Instructions
1. In a medium saucepan, cover the dried apples with warm water and let soak for several hours or overnight.

2. Keeping the same water in the pan, cook the apples over medium heat and bring to a boil. Reduce heat and simmer until tender. Add a bit more water if needed.

3. Preheat oven to 425°F.

4. Puree the apples and the cooking water in a food processor.

5. Mix the sugar and spices into the apple mixture.

6. Pour the mixture into the unbaked pie shell.

7. Moisten the edges with cold water and cover the pie with the top crust. Seal the edges and make a few slices in the top crust to vent.

8. Brush the top with cream and sprinkle with coarse sugar.

9. Bake for 15 minutes. Reduce heat to 350°F and bake for another 30–35 minutes, until top crust is golden brown.

Tip Estes's children watch their mother make a pie near Fowler, Indiana, 1937.

Photograph by Russell Lee, Library of Congress, Prints and Photographs Division.

Speedy Custard Pie

A very hot oven provides a short bake time for this classic custard pie.

Makes 1 pie

Ingredients
1 unbaked pie shell

For the filling:
4 eggs, slightly beaten
1 cup sugar
1/4 teaspoon salt
1 1/2 teaspoons vanilla extract
2 1/2 cups milk
Nutmeg, for dusting

Instructions
1. Preheat oven to 475°F.

2. Scald the milk by warming it on the stove in a saucepan to almost boiling, then remove from heat and let come to room temperature.

3. In a large mixing bowl, thoroughly mix eggs, sugar, vanilla, and salt.

4. Slowly stir in the scalded milk.

5. Immediately pour mixture into the unbaked pie shell.

6. Dust the top of the pie with nutmeg.

7. Bake for 5 minutes, then reduce heat to 425°F and bake an additional 10 minutes, or until a knife inserted halfway between the center and the edge of the pie comes out clean.

8. Cool to set and serve chilled.

Regional Favorites

Door County Belgian Prune Pie

A small group of nineteenth-century Belgian settlers made their home in Door County, Wisconsin, where they served this yeast-raised crust pie at holiday celebrations. The filling consists of a layer of dried fruit cooked in brandy, with a creamy, rice-pudding layer on top.

Makes 1 pie

Ingredients
For the fruit layer:
- 1 cup pitted prunes
- 1/4 cup brandy
- 1/4 cup sugar
- 2 tablespoons water

For the pudding layer:
- 1 cup rice (cooked)
- 4 cups whole milk
- 1/3 cup light brown sugar
- 1/3 cup granulated sugar
- 1/2 teaspoon cinnamon
- 2 1/2 teaspoons vanilla extract
- 4 large eggs

For the crust:
- 1/4 cup warm water
- 2 teaspoons instant yeast
- 1/4 cup sugar
- 2 cups all-purpose flour, plus more for dusting work area
- 1/4 teaspoon salt
- 2 large eggs, separated
- 3 tablespoons butter (melted)
- Nonstick cooking spray

Instructions

1. For the fruit layer, combine all the ingredients in a medium saucepan and cook over medium-low heat for 15–20 minutes, until sugar is dissolved and mixture has thickened. Remove from heat and let cool a few minutes. Transfer the mixture to a food processor and blend to a paste. Place in the refrigerator to continue to cool and thicken.

2. For the pudding layer, combine the cooked rice with the milk, sugars, cinnamon, and vanilla in a medium saucepan and cook over medium-low heat. Simmer for about 40 minutes, until the rice is very soft. Remove from heat.

3. In a large bowl, beat the eggs. Very slowly add in the warm rice mixture, constantly whisking. Once all of the mixture has been added, return the pudding to the saucepan and continue to whisk. Keeping the heat on medium-low, continue to cook the mixture for another 4–5 minutes to thicken. Remove from heat, transfer to a clean bowl, and refrigerate to cool.

4. Begin making the crust by stirring the yeast into the warm water in a small bowl. Sprinkle the sugar on top and let rest for 5 minutes to activate the yeast.

5. In a clean bowl, beat the egg whites until stiff. Beat in the yolks, then the sugar and melted butter.

6. Stir in the activated yeast, then slowly add the flour and salt to create a sticky dough.

7. Prepare your work surface by dusting it with flour. Move the dough from the bowl to your work surface and knead the dough for about 1 minute. Spray a clean bowl with cooking

spray and transfer the dough to the bowl. Cover with plastic wrap and let rise in a warm place until the dough has doubled in size (about 1 hour).

8. Preheat oven to 350°F.

9. Return the dough to your work surface and roll it out into a circle to fit your pie pan. Place the crust into your pie pan. Cover it again and let rise for 10 minutes.

10. Spread the cooled fruit paste over the bottom of the crust.

11. Stir the cooled pudding and spread over the fruit paste.

12. Bake for 45 minutes or until golden.

13. Chill to serve.

The Norske Nook Bakery & Restaurant in Osseo, Wisconsin, settled in 1857, attracts visitors with Scandinavian specialties and award-winning pies.

Photograph in the Carol M. Highsmith Archive, Library of Congress, Prints and Photographs Division.

Illinois Pumpkin Pie

Pumpkin pie wasn't invented in the American Midwest, but it's certainly got a prominent place there today. In 2015, it became the official state pie of Illinois. The choice was fitting. Eighty-five percent of the world's canned pumpkin is packed in the Libby's factory in Morton, and according to the USDA, in 2021, Illinois harvested 15,900 acres of the squash, twice as much as any other US state!

Makes 1 pie

Ingredients
  1 unbaked pie shell

For the filling:
  2 cups canned pumpkin
  2 eggs (well-beaten)
  1 cup sugar
  1 cup milk
  1 tablespoon butter (melted)
  1/2 teaspoon salt
  1 tablespoon ground ginger
  1/2 teaspoon cinnamon
  1 teaspoon baking powder

  Whipped cream for topping

Instructions
1. Preheat oven to 425°F.

2. In a large saucepan, combine all the ingredients and cook over low heat, just long enough to heat through.

3. Pour the filling into the pie shell.

4. Bake for 15 minutes.

5. Reduce heat to 350°F and bake another 45 minutes.

6. Top with whipped cream.

A farmer's roadside display of pumpkins for sale outside his house in Thomson, Illinois, 2019.

Photograph by Carol M. Highsmith, the Carol M. Highsmith Archive, Library of Congress, Prints and Photographs Division.

Michigan Cherry Pie

Northern Michigan is known as the cherry capital of the world. This perfectly sweet and tart pie has a traditional crust with a streusel top.

Makes 1 pie

Ingredients
1 unbaked pie shell

For the filling:
5 cups fresh tart cherries, pitted
1 cup dried cherries
1/2 teaspoon grated lemon zest
1 teaspoon lemon juice
1 cup sugar
1/4 cup cornstarch

For the topping:
3/4 cup old-fashioned oats
1/2 cup flour
1/2 cup brown sugar
1/3 cup butter (melted)
1/4 teaspoon salt

Instructions
1. Preheat oven to 375°F.

2. In a large bowl, mix all the ingredients for the filling.

3. In a separate bowl, mix all the fillings for the topping.

4. Spread the filling into the pie shell. Cover with the topping mixture.

5. Bake 45–55 minutes or until golden.

6. Serve with vanilla ice cream.

Queen of the National Cherry Festival, Eliene Lyon of Traverse City, Michigan, presents a huge cherry pie (a gift to President Eisenhower) to Secretary of State Marvin McIntyre in 1955 in Washington DC.

Photograph by Harris & Ewing, Library of Congress, Prints and Photographs Division.

Navy Bean Pie

A bean pie is a more affordable substitute to pecan pie. While southern African American recipes usually called for pinto beans, this navy bean version became associated with the Nation of Islam, whose strict diet didn't include common pie ingredients such as sweet potatoes or white flour, and which banned all beans except for the navy bean.

Makes 1 pie

Ingredients
    1 unbaked pie shell (whole wheat)

For the filling:
    1/2 cup butter (softened)
    1 1/2 cups brown sugar
    1 tablespoon cinnamon
    1/2 teaspoon nutmeg
    1 tablespoon cornstarch
    1/4 teaspoon salt
    3 eggs
    1 1/2 cups navy beans, cooked and pureed
    1 cup evaporated milk
    1 teaspoon vanilla extract
    1 tablespoon lemon zest

Instructions
1. Preheat oven to 350°F.

2. Cream the butter and sugar in a mixing bowl.

3. Add the spices, cornstarch, and salt and continue mixing.

4. Add the eggs one at a time and continue mixing.

5. Add the beans, mixing to fully combine and until the mixture is smooth.

6. Mix in the evaporated milk, vanilla, and lemon zest.

7. Pour the filling into the pie shell.

8. Cook for 5 minutes, then lower the temperature to 325°F.

9. Cool completely to set.

Ohio Buckeye Pie

Midwesterners know a buckeye candy as a rolled ball of peanut butter and powdered sugar, dipped in melted chocolate, leaving just a circle of the peanut butter revealed so that the candy resembles the nut of a buckeye tree. "Buckeye" is now a universal term for this flavor combination.

Makes 1 pie

Ingredients

For the crumb crust:
- 25 chocolate sandwich cookies
- 5 tablespoons butter (melted)

For the filling:
- 1 8-ounce package cream cheese, softened
- 1 1/2 cups creamy peanut butter
- 1 teaspoon vanilla extract
- 2 cups powdered sugar
- 1/2 cup whipping cream

For the topping:
- 1/2 cup semisweet chocolate chips
- 4 tablespoons whipping cream

Instructions:

1. For the crust, pulse the cookies in the food processor (or roll with a rolling pin in a plastic bag) to turn into crumbs. Mix the melted butter into the crumbs and press into a pie pan. Chill in the refrigerator to set while you make the filling.

2. Beat the cream cheese with an electric mixture.

3. Add the peanut butter and vanilla until combined.

4. Slowly add in the powdered sugar and continue mixing.

5. Add the heavy cream and mix until combined.

6. Spread the mixture into the cookie crust.

7. For the topping, combine the cream and chocolate chips in a microwave-safe bowl. Microwave for 15 seconds, then stir. Continue to microwave in 15-second increments until the chocolate is melted, smooth, and glossy. Allow to cool for a few minutes, then spread the topping onto the peanut butter filling. (Leave a naked circle in the center if you'd like your pie to resemble a giant buckeye!)

8. Chill for several hours to set.

Shaker Lemon Pie

Not your standard diner-case lemon pie, this pie uses entire lemons, thinly sliced and macerated in sugar for a full day (so be sure to plan ahead!). This pie was invented by the Shakers—a religious sect that founded settlements in Ohio and Indiana in the early nineteenth century. The frugality and simplicity of their culture is reflected in this short recipe.

Makes 1 pie

Ingredients
2 unbaked pie crusts

For filling:
2 lemons
2 cups sugar
4 eggs
Pinch of salt

Instructions
1. Slice the lemons as thinly as possible, reserving as much juice as possible.

2. Put the sliced lemons and juice into a bowl and cover with sugar and a pinch of salt. Stir. Let the lemons sit in the refrigerator for at least 8–12 hours.

3. When ready to bake, preheat oven to 450°F.

4. In a medium-sized bowl, whisk the eggs.

5. Brush the bottom pie shell with the beaten eggs.

6. Pour the lemon mixture into the remaining eggs and stir.

7. Pour the mixture into the pie shell. Cover with the second crust, then trim and seal the edges. Cut a few slits in the top crust to vent.

8. Bake for 20 minutes. Cover with foil. Reduce heat to 400°F and bake an additional 15–20 minutes.

A Shaker kitchen, 1933.
Library of Congress, Prints and Photographs Division.

Sour Cream Raisin Pie

This pie is said to have been introduced in the Midwest by German immigrants, but similar recipes have been found in Mennonite and African American community cookbooks. The custard is cooked on the stovetop before being added to the crust, so the oven is only required to set the optional meringue topping.

Makes 1 pie

Ingredients
   1 baked pie shell

   For the filling:
   2 egg yolks
   1 whole egg
   1/4 cup cloves
   1/2 teaspoon cinnamon
   1 cup sour cream
   1/2 cup raisins
   1 teaspoon lemon juice
   1/2 cup sugar

   For the meringue topping (optional):
   2 egg whites

Instructions
1. Preheat oven to 350°F.

2. Beat the eggs lightly.

3. Mix in the sugar, spices, sour cream, and raisins.

4. Cook in a double boiler until thick, stirring constantly

5. When thick, let cool for 10–15 minutes, then pour into the baked pie shell.

6. For the meringue topping, beat 2 egg whites until stiff peaks form. Spread over filling.

7. Bake for 15 minutes until meringue is set and lightly golden.

Win Schuler's Grasshopper Pie

The Schuler family in Marshall, Michigan, has been hosting generations of midwesterners for over a century. The original hotel/restaurant was named for Winston Schuler, who retired in the 1980s. He passed the torch to his son Hans, who rebranded the establishment simply to Schuler's, and who operates the restaurant today. Fortunately, this classic recipe found its way into a few local cookbooks because it's no longer on the menu.

Makes 1 pie

Ingredients
For the crust:
1 1/4 cups crushed chocolate wafer cookies
1/3 cup butter (melted)

For the filling:
2/3 cup milk
24 large marshmallows
2 ounces crème de menthe
1 ounce crème de cocoa
1 cup whipping cream

Whipped cream, sliced strawberries

Instructions
1. Preheat oven to 350°F.

2. To make the crust, combine the cookie crumbs and butter and press into the sides and bottom of a pie pan. Bake for 10 minutes and allow to cool.

3. Scald (heat to almost but not quite boiling) milk over a double boiler.

4. Stir in the marshmallows and mix until melted.

5. Allow to cool.

6. Whip the cream to stiff peaks and fold in the liqueurs.

7. Fold the cream into the marshmallow mixture.

8. Spread the filling into the cookie crust and freeze.

9. Remove from freezer one hour before serving.

10. Garnish with a sliced strawberry or extra whipped cream if desired.

"Desperation" Pies

Buttermilk Pie

This pie recipe was a good way to use up buttermilk—a by-product of making butter at home. The lemon flavoring (you can use real lemon juice if you prefer) enhances the tanginess.

Makes 1 pie

Ingredients
1 unbaked pie shell

For the filling:
2 eggs
1 cup sugar
2 tablespoons flour
2 cups buttermilk
1 teaspoon baking soda
1 teaspoon lemon flavoring

Instructions
1. Preheat oven to 400°F.

2. In a medium bowl, beat the eggs.

3. Stir in the sugar and flour.

4. In a separate bowl, dissolve the baking soda in the buttermilk.

5. Add the buttermilk to the egg mixture, along with the lemon flavoring. Pour into the pie shell.

6. Bake for 10 minutes, then lower the oven temperature to 350°F and bake an additional 30 minutes or until a knife inserted in the center comes out clean.

Chess Pie

This is a rich custard pie made from pantry ingredients for when fruit is scarce. While old chess pie recipes can vary, the common uniting ingredients seem to be cornmeal and vinegar. The name is often debated. One origin story claims that the pie was shelf-stable after baking and could be stored in or under a "chest." Another one suggests that the name came from former enslaved people, who, when asked what type of pie they had made, would respond, "it's *jest* a pie."

Makes 1 pie

Ingredients
1 baked pie shell

For the filling:
4 eggs
2 cups sugar
2 tablespoons cornmeal
1 tablespoon flour
1/4 teaspoon salt
1/2 cup butter (melted)
1/4 cup milk
1 tablespoon vinegar
1 teaspoon vanilla extract

Powdered sugar (for garnish)

Instructions

1. Preheat oven to 350°F.

2. In a large bowl, beat the eggs.

3. Add all the remaining ingredients and mix well.

4. Pour into the baked pie shell.

5. Bake for 15 minutes. Remove from oven and wrap the edges of the pie crust with aluminum foil so that the edges do not get overly brown.

6. Bake for another 40–45 minutes until set.

7. Cool to serve. Garnish with powdered sugar.

Hoosier Pie
(Indiana Sugar Cream Pie)

This simple, sweet, creamy pie is the unofficial state pie of Indiana. Falling into the category of "desperation pies," it's a pie that could be made when money was tight or fresh fruit wasn't available.

Makes 2 pies

Ingredients
2 baked, 9-inch pastry shells

For the filling:
2 cups sugar, separated
3 cups half-and-half
3/4 cup butter
1/4 cup margarine
1/3 cup cornstarch
Pinch of salt

Nutmeg

Instructions
1. Preheat oven to 350°F.

2. In a medium saucepan, bring the half-and-half, 1 1/2 cups sugar, and salt to boiling.

3. In a medium bowl, mix together 1/2 cup sugar and cornstarch. Add the boiling milk mixture gradually to the sugar and cornstarch mixture.

4. Set aside 1 tablespoon of butter. Add the remaining butter and margarine to the sugar mixture.

5. Return the mixture to the saucepan to heat and cook, stirring until thick.

6. Pour into baked shells. Sprinkle with nutmeg and a few dots of the reserved butter.

7. Bake until lightly browned, about 15 minutes.

A family enjoys Christmas dinner in the home of Earl Pauley, near Smithfield, Iowa, in 1936. Dinner consisted of potatoes, cabbage, and pie.

Photograph by Russell Lee, Library of Congress, Prints and Photographs Division.

Mock Apple (Ritz Cracker) Pie

This pie recipe debuted on the back of Ritz Cracker boxes during the Great Depression. The crackers melt into an apple-like filling, while the lemon and cinnamon aid in the deception.

Makes 1 pie

Ingredients
2 unbaked pie shells

For the filling:
36 Ritz Crackers, coarsely broken
1 3/4 cups water
2 cups sugar
2 tablespoons butter
1/2 teaspoon cinnamon
2 teaspoons cream of tartar
2 tablespoons lemon juice
Grated peel of one lemon

Instructions
1. Preheat oven to 425°F.

2. Spread the cracker crumbs into the bottom pie crust.

3. Combine water, sugar, and cream of tartar in a saucepan. Cook over high heat and bring to a boil. Simmer for 15 minutes. Add lemon juice and grated lemon peel.

4. Remove the mixture from the heat and let cool.

5. When cool, pour the mixture over the cracker crumbs in the pie shell.

6. Cut the butter into small pieces, scatter over the filling, then sprinkle with cinnamon.

7. Place the top crust over the filling. Seal and trim the edges. Cut a few slits across the top crust to vent.

8. Bake for 30–35 minutes, until crust is crip and golden.

9. Cool and let set before serving.

Professional cooks showing off a turkey and an impressive array of pies, 1922.

Library of Congress, Prints and Photographs Division.

Shoofly Pie

Shoofly pie was invented by the Pennsylvania Dutch in the nineteenth century. It originated as a crumb cake that was placed in a pie shell for easier eating (without a plate and fork). Traditionally, this pie was eaten as a breakfast food with coffee rather than as a dessert. The molasses adds moisture and acts as a binder in place of eggs, which were omitted due to their lack of availability in the winter. The modern name "shoofly" possibly came from a popular brand of molasses, or because the dark molasses would attract flies as the pie cooled on an open windowsill.

There are two variations of this pie, a "dry-bottom" version that is more fully combined and set like a cake, and this "wet-bottom" version, which features three distinct layers: the pie crust, the gooey molasses layer, and the crumb topping.

Makes 1 pie

Ingredients
1 baked pie shell

For the molasses layer:
1/3 cup molasses
1/2 cup boiling water
1/2 teaspoon baking soda
1 cup flour
1 cup packed brown sugar
1 teaspoon cinnamon
1/4 cup butter (cut in chunks)

Instructions

1. Preheat oven to 350°F.

2. Pour the boiling water into a small bowl and add the baking soda. Stir to combine.

3. Add the molasses to the bowl.

4. In a separate bowl, combine the flour, brown sugar, and cinnamon.

5. Cut the butter into the dry ingredients with your fingers or a pastry cutter to form fine crumbs.

6. Pour the molasses mixture into the pie crust. Mix in about one-third of your crumb mixture.

7. Sprinkle the remaining crumb mixture on top. Do not mix.

8. Bake for about 25 minutes or until set.

Sugar Milk Pie

A bit lighter than a custard pie, this three-ingredient pie filling couldn't be any simpler.

Makes 1 pie

Ingredients
    1 unbaked pie shell

   For the filling:
    2/3 cup sugar
    1/3 cup flour
    2 cups whole milk

Instructions
1. Preheat oven to 350°F.

2. In a medium bowl, combine the sugar and flour, then put the mixture into the pie shell.

3. Add the milk to the pie shell, mixing the ingredients with your fingers.

4. Bake for 40 minutes or until set.

Vinegar Pie

When fruit was in short supply, a tangy vinegar could balance the sweetness in this surprisingly delicious pie. While classic recipes may call for white vinegar and white sugar, the fruitiness of apple cider vinegar and the richness of brown sugar in this recipe create a more familiar pie flavor. Present it as "Apple Cider Pie" to make it more appealing to your guests.

Makes 1 pie

Ingredients
    1 baked pie shell

For the filling:
    4 eggs
    1/4 cup butter (melted)
    1 1/2 cups brown sugar
    2 tablespoons apple cider vinegar
    1 teaspoon vanilla extract
    Pinch of salt

    Whipped cream for garnish

Instructions
1. Preheat oven to 350°F.

2. Whisk the eggs well, then add the remaining ingredients and whisk again.

3. Pour the filling into the baked pie shell and bake for 30–40 minutes until set.

4. Cool to room temperature, then refrigerate to continue setting.

Midwestern
Ingredients

All-American Apple Pie

A book of American pie recipes—midwestern or not—that doesn't include one for apple pie would be, well . . . un-American.

Makes 1 pie

Ingredients
2 unbaked pie crusts

For the filling:
3 1/2 cups peeled and thinly sliced apples
1/2 cup sugar
3 tablespoons golden raisins
3 tablespoons walnuts
1/2 teaspoon cinnamon
1/2 teaspoon grated lemon rind
2 teaspoons lemon juice
1 egg yolk
1 teaspoon water

For the glaze:
1/4 cup powdered sugar
1/2 teaspoon lemon juice

Instructions
1. Preheat oven to 400 °F.

2. In a large bowl, combine the apples, sugar, raisins, walnuts, cinnamon, lemon rind, and juice.

3. Spoon filling into the bottom pie crust. Note: be sure your bottom crust is large enough to hang over the sides of the pie pan because you'll be sealing the lattice-top crust with it in step 9.

4. Use the second crust to make a lattice top by cutting it into strips about 1/2 inch wide. Lay a row of strips horizontally so they are parallel across the pie, about 1/2 inch apart.

5. Fold back (onto itself) every other strip.

6. Place one long strip vertically in the center of the pie. It will only cover the unfolded horizontal strips. Unfold the horizontal folded strips over the center strip.

7. Take the horizontal strips (that you didn't fold the first time) and fold them back onto themselves, laying them on top of the center strip. Place a second vertical strip of dough next to the first strip, with about 1/2 inch between them. Unfold the folded horizontal strips over the second vertical strip.

8. Continue weaving additional vertical strips in the above manner to cover the top of the pie.

9. Trim the edges of the strips with kitchen scissors, leaving enough length to reach the side of the pie plate. Fold over the dough of the bottom crust to cover the edges and scallop crimp to seal.

How to scallop crimp: Scallop crimping creates a pretty, wavy pattern around your pie, while at the same time sealing the top crust to the bottom crust. To crimp the edges, use your index finger to push down on the edge of the pastry, and use the finger and thumb of your other hand to pinch the pastry on either side. That's your first wave. Move your finger to the other side of the wave and repeat. Continue all the way around the rim of the pie pan.

10. Beat the egg yolk with water and gently brush over the top of the pie.

11. Bake for 40–60 minutes. Check the pie after 30 minutes. If the top is browning too much, cover the pie with foil.

12. Cool for one hour.

13. Combine the glaze ingredients and drizzle over the warm pie.

A woman making an apple pie, 1943.
Photograph by John Collier Jr., Library of Congress, Prints and Photographs Division.

Black Walnut Chocolate Pie

If you're out walking in the Midwest in the fall, familiarize yourself with how to identify a black walnut tree. Then look on the ground for this deliciously foraged pie filling. The flavor of a black walnut is fruiter and bolder than a standard English variety. If you forage them rather than buying them bagged and roasted, give yourself a little more time to prep them to enhance the flavor.

Makes 1 pie

Ingredients
1 unbaked pie shell

For the filling:
3 eggs
1 1/2 cups sugar
6 tablespoons butter (melted)
2 teaspoons vanilla extract
3/4 cup flour
1 1/2 cups semisweet chocolate chips
1 1/2 cups chopped black walnuts

Whipped cream or vanilla ice cream for serving

If you've foraged your walnuts, shell and soak the meats in salted water for 6–8 hours or overnight. Drain, then dry in your oven at 150°F for a few hours until they're dehydrated and crisp. This step is not necessarily required but will make the nuts easier to digest, and it will bring out their bold flavor.

Instructions

1. Preheat oven to 350°F.

2. In a large bowl, beat the eggs.

3. Add the sugar, butter, and vanilla. Beat until well blended.

4. Add the flour and mix well.

5. Fold in the chocolate chips and walnuts.

6. Pour the mixture into the baked pie shell.

7. Bake for 1 hour or until a toothpick comes out clean.

8. Serve warm with whipped cream or vanilla ice cream.

Bluebarb Pie

A dreamy fruit combination of—you guessed it—blueberries and rhubarb that is unique to the Midwest.

Makes 1 pie

Ingredients
  2 unbaked pie shells

  For the filling:
  2 cups rhubarb, diced
  2 cups blueberries
  2/3 cup sugar
  4 teaspoons cornstarch
  Pinch of salt

  Cinnamon sugar for dusting the top

Instructions
1. Preheat oven to 425°F.

2. Mix the sugar and cornstarch together well.

3. Sprinkle the mixture over the combined blueberries and rhubarb and let sit for ten minutes.

4. Add the fruit to the bottom pie shell.

5. Make a lattice for the top from the second crust and sprinkle it with cinnamon sugar.

6. Bake for 30 minutes until the crust is well browned and the fruit is thickly bubbling in the center.

Blueberry Cream Pie

The cream in this pie is *sour* cream, which creates a rich, sweet custard that holds the tart blueberries.

Makes 1 pie

Ingredients
1 unbaked pie shell

For the filling:
- 1 cup sugar
- 1 cup sour cream
- 3 tablespoons flour
- 1/4 teaspoon salt
- 4 cups blueberries

For the crumb topping:
- 1/3 cup butter (cold)
- 1/2 cup flour
- 1/4 cup sugar

Instructions
1. Preheat oven to 375°F.

2. Combine sugar, sour cream, flour, and salt.

3. Spread the berries into the pie shell.

4. Spread the sour cream topping over the berries.

5. For the crumb topping, sift the flour and the sugar. Mix in the butter with your fingers until combined and crumbly. Sprinkle over the top of the pie.

6. Bake for 40–45 minutes.

A man distributes slices of pie to young contestants in a pie-eating contest at a 4-H club fair in 1939. Suprisingly, the first recorded pie-eating contest was held in Toronto, Canada, in 1878. However, the trend spread quickly throughout the United States, where the contests were often held at county fairs.

Photograph by Russell Lee, Library of Congress, Prints and Photographs Division.

Chokecherry Pie

Chokecherries are tiny, red, very tart berries that grow on small trees throughout the Midwest. They have a long history of use among Indigenous people, and they are North Dakota's official state fruit. This recipe calls only for the juice of the chokecherry. If you're foraging your own chokecherries, you'll want to make your own juice first by washing, boiling, then thoroughly straining them so you do not include any stems, pits, or skins. Be warned that the pits and foliage are poisonous. One pound of berries will result in about 1 cup of juice.

Makes 1 pie

Ingredients
    2 unbaked pie shells

    For the filling:
    2 1/2 cups chokecherry juice
    1/2 cup sugar
    4 tablespoons cornstarch
    1/8 teaspoon salt
    1 egg

Instructions
1. Preheat oven to 425°F.

2. In a medium saucepan, combine the juice, sugar, almond extract, cornstarch, and salt.

3. Cook over low to medium heat until thickened.

4. Let cool and pour into pie shell.

5. Create a lattice top with the second pie crust. Crimp the edges to seal.

6. Beat the egg and brush the top crust and edges.

7. Cover the pie edges with foil to prevent over-browning, and bake for 25 minutes. Place a baking sheet on the rack below to catch any overflow. Remove foil, lower oven temperature to 400°F, and bake an additional 15–20 minutes.

8. Cool to set.

Concord Grape Pie

The arrival of Concord grapes at markets in the Midwest is bittersweet, announcing summer's end. The over-the-top grapey flavor of Concord grapes is nothing like that of everyday grocery store red or white grapes, so don't attempt to make any substitutions. And give yourself some time; the separation of the flesh from the skins and seeds takes some patience.

Makes 1 pie

Ingredients
   1 unbaked pie shell

For the filling:
   4 cups Concord grapes
   1 cup sugar
   1/4 cup enriched flour
   1/4 teaspoon salt
   1 tablespoon lemon juice
   1 1/2 teaspoons butter (melted)

For the crumb topping:
   1/3 cup butter (cold)
   1/2 cup flour
   1/4 cup sugar

Instructions
1. Preheat oven to 450°F.

2. Slip the skins off the grapes by squeezing each one with your fingers. Set the skins aside—you'll be adding them back into the filling later.

3. In a saucepan over medium heat, gently mash the grapes to release the juices and cook to a boil. Simmer for 5 minutes. Gently mash the grapes to release the juices.

4. Remove from the heat and cool the grapes enough to safely press them through a sieve to remove the seeds. Use the back of a wooden spoon to help press the grape pulp through the sieve. Discard the seeds.

5. Add the skins back into the grape pulp, along with the sugar, flour, salt, lemon juice, and melted butter.

6. Pour the mixture into the pie shell.

7. For the crumb topping, sift the flour and the sugar. Mix in the butter with your fingers until combined and crumbly. Sprinkle over the top of the pie.

8. Place a cookie sheet on the rack below your pie to catch any overflow and bake for 15–20 minutes.

Fresh Strawberry Pie

Using Bisquick for a pie crust is a fast and easy substitute that is quite popular in midwestern community cookbooks. This crust can really handle any type of filling, be it sweet or savory.

Makes 1 pie

Ingredients
For the crust:
1 cup Bisquick
3 tablespoons boiling water
1/4 cup butter (softened)

For the filling:
1 quart strawberries
3 tablespoons cornstarch
1 cup water
1 cup sugar

Instructions
1. Preheat oven to 450°F.

2. Mix the crust ingredients in a pie pan until a dough forms. Pat the dough to the edges of the pan.

3. Bake 8–10 minutes and cool.

4. Stem and slice the strawberries.

5. In a saucepan, add one cup of the berries (pick the smaller or misshapen ones first) with 2/3 cup of water, and mash.

6. Bring to a boil and cook until strawberries darken.

7. In a small bowl, dissolve the cornstarch and sugar in the remaining water, then add to the berries.

8. Pour the berries into the baked pie crust.

9. Refrigerate a minimum of two hours to set. Serve with whipped cream or vanilla ice cream.

A woman adds her donation to the table at a pie auction in McIntosh County, Oklahoma, 1940.

Photograph by Russell Lee, Library of Congress, Prints and Photographs Division.

Manoomin (Wild Rice) Pie

Manoomin is a highly nutritious wild rice, known as a sacred food to the Lake Superior Ojibwe Tribe. You can substitute with any wild rice in this recipe, but specialty companies in the Midwest, such as the Minnesota-based Native Harvest, do sell the ancient grain online.

While this pie is similar to a pecan pie, adding the popped rice topping makes it unique.

Makes 1 pie

Ingredients
1 unbaked pie shell

For the topping:
1/4 cup wild rice
Oil to fill the bottom of a small saucepan about 1/2 inch deep

For the filling:
3 eggs and 1 egg yolk
1 cup white sugar
3 tablespoons brown sugar
1/2 teaspoon salt
1 cup corn syrup
3/4 teaspoon vanilla extract
1/4 cup butter (melted)

1 heaping cup of cooked wild rice

Instructions

1. Preheat oven to 350°F.

2. For the topping, heat the oil in a small saucepan. Put the uncooked rice into a small sieve that fits fully into the pan. When the oil is hot, carefully dip the rice into the oil to completely submerge. The rice should puff up pretty quickly, no longer than 30 seconds. When it's popped, remove from the hot oil and drain on a paper towel.

3. For the filling, beat the eggs in a large bowl.

4. Mix in the sugars, salt, corn syrup, vanilla, and butter.

5. Spread the cooked (not popped) wild rice into the bottom of the pie shell.

6. Spread the popped rice on top of the cooked rice.

7. Pour the filling mixture on top of the rice. The popped rice will float to the top when baking.

8. Bake for 50–60 minutes until only the center is slightly jiggly.

9. Cool to serve.

Maple Syrup Pie

Only four ingredients are needed for this pie's filling, so take the time to have extra dough on hand to decorate the top with cutouts. A maple-leaf cookie cutter would be perfect, but really any shape will do.

Makes 1 pie

Ingredients
    1 unbaked pie shell
    Additional unbaked pie dough or shell for top cutouts (optional)

  For the filling:
    3 tablespoons cornstarch
    2/3 cup water
    1 1/2 cups maple syrup
    2 tablespoons butter

Instructions
1. Preheat oven to 400°F.

2. In a large saucepan, combine the water, maple syrup, and cornstarch. Cook over medium heat and bring to a boil.

3. Reduce heat and simmer for about 5 minutes until smooth and thickened.

4. Stir in the butter until melted and fully combined. Remove from heat and cool.

5. Pour the filling into the crust and bake for 10 minutes.

6. Reduce heat to 350°F and bake for an additional 35–40 minutes, or until filling is bubbling and crust is brown.

7. While pie is cooling, roll out the additional pie dough on a floured surface to 1/4-inch thickness. Make cutout shapes with a cookie cutter and bake on a baking sheet for about 10 minutes.

8. Place cutout shapes on top of pie before serving.

A migrant family of seven shares a lunch of a single pie alongside the highway east of Fort Gibson, Oklahoma, 1939.
Photograph by Russell Lee, Library of Congress, Prints and Photographs Division.

Peach Polka-Dot Pie

This recipe calls for a "mix in the pan" pie crust, which means there's no need to roll out dough. The peaches are simply halved rather than sliced, not covered by a top crust as in a traditional peach pie, creating charming large polka dots in the dish.

Makes 1 pie

Ingredients

For the crust:
  1 cup + 2 tablespoons flour
  1 tablespoon sugar
  1/4 teaspoon salt
  1/3 cup vegetable oil
  1 1/2 tablespoons milk

For the filling:
  6 peaches
  1/4 cup flour
  3/4 cup sugar
  2 teaspoons cinnamon
  1 cup whipping cream

Instructions

1. Preheat the oven to 425°F.

2. For the crust, mix the flour, sugar, and salt into a nongreased pie pan.

3. In a separate bowl, mix the oil and milk.

4. Add the dry ingredients in the pie pan and mix well. Press the mixture into the pie pan to form the crust. Bake for 5 minutes until set.

5. For the filling, carefully peel, pit, and halve the peaches, keeping their half-globe shape as much as possible.

6. Set the peaches on the pie crust with the cut side down in a pleasing arrangement.

7. In a separate bowl, combine the flour, sugar, and cinnamon.

8. Add the (unwhipped) whipping cream and blend well.

9. Pour the mixture over the peaches.

10. Bake for 45 minutes or until the custard is set.

11. Cool before serving.

Pecan Oatmeal Pie

This is a cross between a pecan pie and a chewy oatmeal cookie. Adding a touch of honey to the whipped cream is a welcome surprise.

Makes 1 pie

Ingredients
1 unbaked pie shell

For the filling:
1/4 cup butter (soft)
1/2 cup brown sugar
1/2 teaspoon cinnamon
1/2 teaspoon cloves
1/4 teaspoon salt
1 cup dark corn syrup
1 cup quick rolled oats
1 cup pecans for the top

1 cup whipping cream
1 teaspoon honey

Instructions
1. Preheat oven to 350°F.

2. In a large bowl, mix the butter and brown sugar.

3. Stir in the cinnamon, cloves, salt, and corn syrup.

4. Stir in the oats.

5. Spread the filling into the unbaked pie shell. Arrange the pecans on the top.

6. Bake for 1 hour.

7. When ready to serve, whip the cream with the honey until peaks form. Top each slice with a dollop of whipped cream.

A truck from the Liberty Pie Company has an unfortunate crash, 1926. The orignal version of our present-day food trucks, pie trucks (and even before that, pie wagons) sold daytime meals to immigrant workers.
Library of Congress, Prints and Photographs Division.

Persimmon Chiffon Pie

American persimmon trees have a long history in the Midwest, dating back to the Indigenous Americans who sought them out for their beautiful, yellow-orange fruit. Persimmons ripen in early fall. After being picked or purchased, let them ripen on your counter until they are quite soft so they are as sweet as possible. If you are lucky enough to find the fruit jarred, canned, or frozen at a local market or orchard, you can save yourself the step of making the pulp.

Makes 1 pie

Ingredients
1 baked pie shell

For the persimmon pulp:
8–12 persimmons, depending on size—enough to equal 2 cups. Lean toward the higher number if you are concerned about how much pulp you'll get. It's better to have extra pulp, which you can then freeze and use for smoothies or to spread on bread like jam.

For filling:
4 egg yolks
1/2 cup sugar
Juice of 2 lemons
1 package of unflavored gelatin, dissolved in 1/3 cup water

For meringue:
4 egg whites
1/2 cup sugar

1 cup whipping cream, for topping

Instructions

1. To make the persimmon pulp, cut off the stems of the fruit and scoop out the flesh and juices from the skin. Remove any seeds if you find them. Blend in a food processor until it is the consistency of applesauce. The riper the fruit, the easier it will be to blend. If needed, add a bit of water to the processor to assist in blending. Transfer pulp and juices to a saucepan and bring to a boil over medium heat. Reduce heat and simmer until fruit is tender. Let cool.

2. In a double boiler, mix the beaten egg yolks, sugar, and lemon juice. Cook, while stirring, until thick.

3. Add dissolved gelatin to the egg and sugar mixture.

4. Add the persimmon pulp to the mixture.

5. Remove from the heat and chill.

6. While chilling, make a meringue by beating 4 egg whites until they are stiff and glossy, adding a little sugar at a time.

7. When the fruit mixture is partially set, fold in the meringue.

8. Spread the filling into the baked pie shell.

9. Chill in the refrigerator until fully set. Top with whipped cream.

Rhubarb Custard Pie

The addition of orange juice concentrate to this filling adds sweetness and familiarity to the tart rhubarb, making this pie more appealing to folks who may be new to the vegetable's flavor.

Makes 1 pie

Ingredients
1 baked pie shell

For the filling:
1 cup sugar
3 tablespoons flour
1/4 teaspoon salt
3 egg yolks
2 tablespoons orange juice concentrate
2 tablespoons butter (melted)
3 cups fresh rhubarb cut into 1/2-inch pieces
1/2 cup chopped pecans
3 egg whites
1/2 cup sugar

Instructions
1. Preheat the oven to 325°F.

2. In a large bowl, combine 1 cup sugar, flour, and salt.

3. Add the egg yolks, orange juice concentrate, and melted butter and beat until smooth.

4. Stir in the rhubarb.

5. In a separate bowl, beat the egg whites until stiff peaks form.

6. Gently fold the egg whites into the rhubarb mixture.

7. Pour the mixture into the baked pie crust and sprinkle with pecans.

8. Bake for 55 minutes.

Zucchini Pie

This is a sweet pie—it's similar in flavor to apple pie—that's a great way to use up summer's bounty from your garden.

Makes 1 pie

Ingredients
For the crumb crust:
3/4 cup butter (cold and cubed)
2 cups flour
1/2 cup sugar
1/2 teaspoon cinnamon

For the filling:
4 cups zucchini, peeled and sliced
1/2 cup lemon juice
1/2 cup sugar
1/2 teaspoon cinnamon
1/8 teaspoon nutmeg

Instructions
1. Preheat oven to 375°F. Grease a pie pan.

2. For the crust, mix all ingredients together. Set aside 1/4 cup, which will be used to thicken the filling later.

3. Pat half of the crust mixture into the pie pan. Bake for 10 minutes.

4. For the filling, cook the zucchini in the lemon juice on the stove top until tender but not mushy.

5. Stir the sugar, cinnamon, and nutmeg and cook 5 more minutes until the sugar is dissolved.

6. Stir in the reserved 1/4 cup of crumb-crust mixture. Cook until thickened.

7. Spread filling over the baked crust. Top with remaining crumb-crust topping.

8. Bake for 30 minutes.

Retro
Favorites

Banana Cream Pie

In the nineteenth century, scientists discovered ways to synthesize flavor chemicals (natural and artificial) to evoke familiar flavors. These flavorings started being added to all sorts of shortcut pie fillings (pudding, Jell-O, bottled extracts). If you're wary of imitation banana flavoring, look for an all-natural version or simply omit it from the recipe and add an extra real banana.

Makes 1 pie

Ingredients
   1 baked pie shell

For the filling:
   1/2 cup sugar
   1/4 teaspoon salt
   4 tablespoons flour
   1 1/2 cups milk
   3 egg yolks
   1/2 teaspoon vanilla
   1 teaspoon banana flavoring
   1 banana

For the meringue:
   1 tablespoon cornstarch
   2 tablespoons cold water
   1/2 cup boiling water
   3 egg whites
   6 tablespoons sugar
   1/4 teaspoon salt

Instructions

1. Preheat oven to 375°F.

2. In a large bowl, combine the sugar, flour, and salt.

3. Stir in the milk, vanilla, and banana flavoring.

4. Cook in a double boiler until thick.

5. In a separate bowl, beat the egg yolks. Add 1/4 cup of the warm mixture to the yolks, then return the eggs to the double boiler and cook for two minutes.

6. Allow to cool, then pour half of the filling into the pie shell.

7. Slice the banana and place on top of the custard. Cover with remaining filling.

8. To make the meringue, dissolve the cornstarch in the cold water. Once dissolved, add the boiling water, then allow to cool.

9. Beat the egg whites until thick. Gradually add the sugar, salt, and vanilla. Continue to beat until stiff peaks form.

10. Fold in the cornstarch mixture.

11. Spread the meringue on top of the filling.

12. Bake to set the meringue, just until golden brown.

Chocolate Marshmallow Pie

This no-bake, kid-friendly recipe appears again and again in community cookbooks under different names—"S'mores Pie," "Hershey Pie," "Candy Bar Pie," or simply just "Chocolate Pie."

Makes 1 pie

Ingredients
1 graham cracker crust

For the filling:
1 7-ounce Hershey Giant chocolate bar (or regular-size bars to equal roughly the same amount)
2/3 cup milk
12 large marshmallows
1 cup heavy cream

Instructions
1. Melt the chocolate in a double boiler until smooth.

2. Mix in the milk and marshmallows.

3. When smooth and fully combined, remove from the heat and let cool.

4. Whip the cream until stiff peaks form, then fold into the cooled chocolate mixture.

5. Pour the filling into the graham cracker crust.

6. Chill for a minimum of two hours. Serve with additional whipped cream if desired.

Chocolate Rum Pie

This pie has a pecan nut crust and a dash of rum in both the crust and the filling. It's a good one to make ahead of time and store in the freezer until ready to serve.

Makes 1 pie

Ingredients
For the crust:

    2 cups pecans, finely chopped
    5 tablespoons brown sugar
    5 tablespoons butter (chilled and cubed)
    2 teaspoons dark rum

For the filling:

    6 ounces of semisweet chocolate chips
    1/2 teaspoon instant espresso powder
    4 eggs
    1 tablespoon dark rum
    1 teaspoon vanilla
    1 cup heavy cream, whipped

    1/2 cup heavy cream, whipped, for topping

Instructions

1. For the crust, blend all the ingredients (with a fork or pastry cutter, or pulse in a food processor) and press into the bottom and sides of a pie pan. Freeze for one hour.

2. For the filling, melt the chocolate in a double boiler.

3. Stir in the espresso powder.

4. In a large bowl, beat the eggs with about 2 tablespoons of the chocolate mixture.

5. Return the beaten egg mixture to the chocolate mixture and stir in the vanilla and rum, whisking over low heat until smooth.

6. Cool for 5 minutes.

7. Whip 1 cup of the heavy cream into stiff peaks. Fold into the cooled chocolate mixture.

8. Pour into the graham cracker crust and freeze.

9. Remove from freezer 1 hour before serving and top with remaining whipped cream.

Cottage Cheese Pie

Serious Eats deems this pie, "a specialty of grandmothers across the Midwest," and that's exactly where this recipe was found—handwritten on a piece of paper and stuck with yellowed tape into a worn and beloved grandmother's notebook of favorite recipes from family, friends, newspapers, and packaging boxes.

Makes 1 pie

Ingredients
1 graham cracker crust

For the filling:
3 eggs, separated
3/4 cup sugar
1/4 teaspoon salt
1 teaspoon vanilla extract
2 tablespoons cornstarch
1 cup milk
1 16-ounce tub of cottage cheese
1 small (8-ounce) can crushed pineapple, drained

Instructions
1. Preheat oven to 350°F.

2. Beat the egg yolks. Reserve the egg whites.

3. Beat in the sugar, salt, vanilla, cornstarch, and milk.

4. Fold in the cottage cheese and pineapple.

5. Beat the egg whites to stiff peaks and fold into the filling.

6. Pour the filling into the graham cracker crust.

7. Bake for 1 hour.

8. Cool to serve.

Men gather around pies set on a Coca-Cola cooler, during a wheat harvest in Nebraska, 1959.

Photograph by Warren K. Leffler, Library of Congress, Prints and Photographs Division.

Cranberry Velvet Pie

This recipe transforms a humble can of cranberry sauce into a festive, fluffy, frozen centerpiece. No baking required.

Makes 1 pie

Ingredients
For the crust:
   1 1/4 cups crushed vanilla wafers
   6 tablespoons butter (melted)

For the filling:
   1 8-ounce package of cream cheese (softened)
   1 cup whipping cream
   1/4 cup sugar
   1/2 teaspoon vanilla extract
   1 16-ounce can of cranberry sauce (whole cranberries)

Additional whipped cream for garnish

Instructions
1. Mix wafer crumbs with melted butter and press firmly into a pie pan to form the crust. Chill in the refrigerator to firm up.

2. In a large bowl, beat the cream cheese with an electric mixer until fluffy.

3. In a separate bowl, beat the whipping cream with the sugar and vanilla until thick but not quite stiff.

4. Gradually add the whipped cream to the cream cheese, beating until smooth and creamy.

5. Fold the cranberries into the cream mixture, setting a few aside for decorating the top of the pie.

6. Spoon the mixture into the crust and freeze until firm (1–2 hours).

7. Remove from freezer 10 minutes before serving. Top with more whipped cream and the reserved cranberries.

Heavenly Fluff Pie

A lemon showstopper worthy of any midwestern diner's pie case.

Makes 1 pie

Ingredients
1 baked pie shell

For the filling:
4 egg yolks
1/4 teaspoon salt
2 teaspoons grated lemon rind
1/2 cup lemon juice
1/2 cup sugar
1 packet unflavored gelatin dissolved in 1/4 cup water

For meringue:
4 egg whites
1/2 cup sugar

1/2 cup whipped cream
Toasted coconut flakes for topping

Instructions
1. Beat the egg yolks.

2. Add the salt, lemon rind, lemon juice, and sugar, and cook in a double boiler until thickened (about 5–10 minutes).

3. Add the dissolved gelatin and let cool.

4. In a separate bowl, beat the egg whites, slowly adding the sugar until stiff and glossy.

5. Fold the egg whites into the lemon custard.

6. Spread the mixture into the pie shell.

7. Cool to set. Top with whipped cream and toasted coconut.

Pineapple Refrigerator Pie

No need to turn on the oven on hot summer days when making a refrigerator pie! A quick graham cracker crust and canned pineapple made this pie based on pantry ingredients a popular weeknight dessert. This recipe does include an uncooked egg, so if you're wary of that, you can substitute an egg replacement.

Makes 1 pie

Ingredients
For the crust:
   20 graham crackers
   1/3 cup butter (melted)

For the filling:
   1/2 cup butter (softened)
   1 cup powdered sugar
   1 egg
   1 cup whipping cream
   1 20-ounce can crushed pineapple

Instructions
1. Crush the graham crackers in a plastic bag with a rolling pin or in a blender.

2. Mix the graham cracker crumbs with the melted butter. Set aside 1/2 cup of the mixture to sprinkle on top of the pie when it is assembled. Press the remaining mixture into your pie pan.

3. In a medium bowl, cream the softened butter and sugar, beating well. Add the egg and continue beating until creamy.

4. Smooth the mixture into the crust.

5. In a clean bowl, beat the whipping cream to stiff peaks.

6. Fold in the pineapple and spread on top of the first layer of the pie.

7. Sprinkle the remaining graham cracker crumbs on top of the pie and chill for at least 6 hours.

A woman stands by a new refrigerator and pours out cold drinks for her children, 1959.

Photograph by John T. Bledsoe, Library of Congress, Prints and Photographs Division.

Self-Frosting Lemon Pie

When this pie is baked, the egg whites rise to the top, creating their own "frosting" and saving you time from making a separate topping. Of course, don't expect a tall fluffy meringue to magically appear. The finished pie is flatter with a pretty, caramelized topping.

Makes 1 pie

Ingredients
   1 unbaked pie shell, frozen
   1 egg white

   For the filling:
   1 tablespoon flour
   1 cup sugar
   2 eggs (separate whites from yolks)
   Juice of 1 lemon
   1 lemon rind, grated
   1 cup boiling water

Instructions
1. Preheat oven to 350°F.

2. Lightly beat one egg white and brush the frozen crust. This will prevent the crust from getting soggy when the warm filling is added.

3. In a large bowl, beat the egg yolks. Add the lemon juice and rind.

4. Mix in the sugar, then the flour.

5. Beat the egg whites in a separate bowl until stiff peaks form. Gently fold into the lemon filling.

6. Pour in the boiling water and stir. Do not overmix.

7. Pour the filling into the crust.

8. Bake for 30–35 minutes.

9. Cool to set and serve.

Sky-High Strawberry Pie

Sky-high (or mile-high) pies are a favorite in midwestern community cookbooks. The large number of fresh strawberries in this recipe—some mashed and some remaining intact—impressively towers high above the pie crust.

Makes 1 pie

Ingredients
1 baked pie shell. Because this pie has a *lot* of filling, a deep-dish pie pan with a 10-inch crust works best.

For the filling:
3 quarts of fresh strawberries, stemmed and hulled
1 1/2 cups sugar
6 tablespoons cornstarch
2/3 cup water
1 cup heavy cream
1 1/2 tablespoons instant vanilla pudding mix

Instructions
1. In a large bowl, mash enough strawberries to equal 3 cups.

2. In a saucepan over medium heat, combine the sugar, cornstarch, mashed berries, and water. Mix well and bring to a boil, stirring constantly.

3. Cook for 2 minutes at boiling and remove from heat.

4. Chill for 20 minutes, stirring occasionally.

5. Mixture will still be slightly warm. Fold in the remaining strawberries.

6. Pile the mixture into the pie shell and chill for 2–3 hours.

7. When ready to serve, whip the heavy cream until soft peaks form. Sprinkle in the powdered pudding mix and continue to whip until stiff. Pipe the whipped cream around the edges of the pie.

Members of the Woman's Christian Temperance Union enjoy coffee and pie after a meeting held in the high school to promote the sale of defense stamps and bonds in Epping, North Dakota, 1942.

Photograph by John Vachon, Library of Congress, Prints and Photographs Division.

Star-Spangled Cherry Pie

The arrival of prepackaged foods created shortcuts in the kitchen, but boxes and can labels also allowed companies to advertise by offering customers recipes that required particular products. These recipes had catchy marketing-style names that caught on and made their way into many recipe boxes and community cookbooks.

Makes 1 pie

Ingredients
    1 graham cracker crust

For the filling:
    1 8-ounce package of cream cheese (softened)
    1 14-ounce can sweetened condensed milk
    1/2 cups bottled lemon juice
    1 teaspoon vanilla
    1 21-ounce can of cherry pie filling

Instructions
1. In a stand mixer, beat the cream cheese until fluffy.

2. Add the milk and continue to blend.

3. Stop the mixer, stir in the lemon juice and vanilla.

4. Pour the cheese mixture into the pie crust.

5. Spread the cherry pie filling on top.

6. Refrigerate for at least 2 hours to set.

Handheld
Pies

Amish Fry Pie

These sweet, moon-shaped handheld pies can be found at bakeries and roadside stands throughout Amish communities in the Midwest. Traditionally, they are pressed together with a special tool called a "fry pie crimper"—look for one in a thrift store while you're on your trip to Amish Country—but sealing them with a fork will also work. Any standard pie crust dough recipe would most likely work here, but this recipe includes a traditional Amish crust. Popular fry pie fillings are apple or schnitz pie filling (page 45).

Makes 20 hand pies

Ingredients

For the dough:
   7 cups flour
   1 1/2 teaspoons baking powder
   2 teaspoons salt
   2 teaspoons sugar
   1 1/2 cups lard, butter, or shortening (cut into chunks)
   2 eggs, beaten
   13 ounces evaporated milk

For the filling:
   6 cups prepared or homemade pie filling (chilled)

For the glaze:
   2 cups powdered sugar
   1 teaspoon vanilla
   4 tablespoons milk

   Vegetable oil for frying

Instructions

1. In a large bowl, mix the flour, baking powder, salt, and sugar.

2. Add your fat of choice and blend it into the dry ingredients with a pastry cutter, fork, or your fingers. Mix well enough to form pea-sized crumbs.

3. In a separate bowl, beat the eggs with the evaporated milk.

4. Slowly add the eggs and milk to the crumbs and bring the dough together in a ball.

5. Pull off enough dough to make a ball the size of a golf ball. Roll out the small ball into a circular pie crust's shape and thickness. It should be about 6 inches in diameter. If you have trouble rolling out a circle, use a 6-inch round cookie cutter to help get the shape.

6. Scoop about 1/3 cup of pie filling onto half of the small crust, keeping the other half empty.

7. Fold the empty side over the filled side. Moisten the edges and seal with a fork to make a half-moon shape.

8. Set aside and repeat steps 5–7 until your fry pies are assembled.

9. Make your glaze by beating the ingredients in a bowl. Set aside.

10. In a large pot, heat the oil to 350°F. Using a slotted spoon, carefully lower the fry pie into the oil. Fry until golden (roughly 3 minutes).

11. Place on a cookie sheet lined with a paper towel to drain.

12. Drizzle the glaze over the fry pies while they are still warm.

Amish fry pies being made inside the farmhouse at Yoder's Amish Home, 2016.

Runza

Unique to Nebraska, this handheld meat pie has a yeasted crust rather than a pie crust, like the Upper Peninsula pasty or Amish fry pie. Some may consider this humble on-the-go meal more of a sandwich and, therefore, a controversial choice for this book, but its origins are similar to the other hand pies included here—in this case, immigrants from Central and Eastern Europe who settled in the Midwest. Despite this history, the name Runza was able to be trademarked by a Nebraskan fast-food franchise, which opened its first store in 1949 and now has multiple locations throughout the Midwest.

Makes 12 runza

Ingredients

For the dough:
- 2 cups milk
- 1/3 cup butter
- 1/4 cup sugar + plus 1 tablespoon sugar
- 1 package dry yeast
- 5 cups flour divided into 3-cup and 2-cup portions
- 1 teaspoon baking powder
- 1/2 teaspoon baking soda
- 1 egg
- 1 teaspoon salt

For the filling:
- 1 pound ground beef
- 2 white onions (diced)
- 4 cups cabbage (shredded)
- 2 tablespoons butter
- Salt and pepper to taste

Instructions

1. To make the dough, warm the milk in a saucepan on the stove to just before boiling. Stir in the butter and sugar. Remove from heat.

2. When the milk cools to the temperature of a warm bath (around 110°F), sprinkle the yeast on top, stir, and let sit.

3. In a large bowl, sift together 3 cups of the flour, the baking powder, and the baking soda.

4. Slowly add the milk mixture to the bowl and beat for about 2 minutes. Cover with plastic wrap and set aside to rise for 30 minutes.

5. After 30 minutes, beat the egg and salt until foamy and add to the dough. Gradually stir in the remaining 2 cups of flour to form a soft dough.

6. On a floured work surface, knead the dough for 5 minutes, then transfer to an oiled bowl. Cover with plastic wrap and let rest again while you make the filling.

7. For the filling, cook the ground meat with the onions in a skillet over medium heat. When the meat is browned and the onion is transparent, drain off the grease and put the mixture into a large bowl.

8. In the same skillet, melt the butter and sauté the cabbage until soft.

9. Add the cabbage to the meat mixture. Add salt and pepper and stir. Taste the cooked filling, then add salt and pepper as needed.

10. Roll the dough out onto a flat surface. Roll to a large rectangle, 1/4-inch thickness. If you don't have a large work area, you may want to start with just rolling out half the dough, keeping the remaining half covered and chilling in the refrigerator.

11. Cut the dough into 6-by-6-inch squares using a sharp knife or pastry cutter.

12. Scoop 1/3 cup of the filling into the center of each square.

13. To close the runza, pinch all four corners of the dough to the center, like a purse. They will be rounded and taller than your finished product at this point.

14. Line a baking sheet with parchment paper. Flip the runza over and place on the baking sheet, folded side down.

15. Preheat oven to 350°F while the runza rise for another 20 minutes.

16. Bake for 20–30 minutes, until golden.

UP (Upper Peninsula) Pasty

These savory handheld pies are popular in northern Michigan's Upper Peninsula region. The area's copper mines drew workers from Cornwall, England, in the early 1800s, who would bring with them this simple, portable lunch. The fillings consisted of whatever meat was available (beef or pork) and root vegetables. The seasonings were kept simple—just salt and pepper—and today, they are served with a side of ketchup or gravy. Your favorite pie crust dough should work for this recipe, but most traditional UP pasty recipes seem to call for a hot-water crust.

Makes 12 pasties

Ingredients

For the dough:
   2 cups shortening
   2 cups boiling water
   6 cups flour
   1 teaspoon salt

For the filling:
   3 large potatoes (cubed)
   1 medium onion (diced)
   1 rutabaga (cubed)
   3 carrots (shredded)
   1 pound lean ground beef
   3/4 pound lean ground pork
   2 teaspoons black pepper
   2 teaspoons salt
   1/4 cup butter
   1 egg, beaten

Instructions

1. Preheat oven to 350°F.

2. In a large bowl, mix the shortening with the hot water until melted.

3. Slowly stir in the flour and salt until a soft dough forms. Refrigerate for 1–2 hours.

Puddy's Pasties on Route 2, Iron Mountain, Michigan, 1988. While this shop no longer exists, many others still do along the Pasty Trail in the Upper Peninsula. A blogger that goes by "The Pasty Guy" (thepastyguy.com) offers travelers maps, reviews, and tips on his site.

4. In a large bowl, crumble the meat and combine with the remaining filling ingredients, except for the butter.

5. Divide the dough into 12 portions.

6. Roll out each portion into a circle.

7. Scoop about 1 1/2–2 cups of filling onto half of the crust, keeping the other half empty. Depending on the size of your vegetables, you may have more filling than you need, so be careful not to overfill.

8. Fold the empty side over the filled side. Moisten the edges and seal with a fork to make a half-moon shape.

9. Set aside and repeat steps 5–7 until your fry pies are assembled.

10. Place the pasties on a baking sheet. Make 3 small slices on each of the top crusts to vent. Brush tops with beaten egg.

11. Bake for about 1 hour, until golden brown.

RECOMMENDED READING

Anastopoulo, Rossi. *Sweet Land of Liberty: A History of America in 11 Pies*, Harry N. Abrams, 2002.

Asquith, Pamela Z.. *Pamela Z. Asquith's Sweet & Savory Pies*, Harmony Book/New York, 1985.

Davidson, Louise. *Pie: Forgotten Recipes*, The Cookbook Publisher, 2022.

Ludwinski, Linda. *Sister Pie: The Recipes & Stories of a Big-Hearted Bakery in Detroit*. Lorena Jones Books, 2018.

McDermott, Kate. *Art of The Pie: A Practical Guide to Homemade Crusts, Fillings, and Life*. The Countryman Press, 2016.

Swell, Barbara. *The Lost Art of Pie Making Made Easy*, Native Ground Books & Music, Inc., 2004.

Thiellen, Amy. *The New Midwestern Table*. Clarkson Potter, 2013.

A young girl eating pie in Detroit, Michigan, 1899.
Donald Roberts, Library of Congress, Prints and Photographs Division.

ABOUT THE AUTHORS

Meredith Pangrace is a designer and food enthusiast from Cleveland, Ohio. She is the editor of *Rust Belt Vegan Kitchen* and has designed books for Belt Publishing since 2013.

Phoebe Mogharei is Belt Publishing's publicity and marketing director. When she moved away from home, her midwestern mother set her up with a multipage document explaining how to make a pie crust in painful detail. Her writing has appeared in the *Chicago Reader*, *Electric Literature*, *Chicago Review of Books*, and *Chicago* magazine.